Bended bias
APPLIQUÉ

Linda M. Poole

American Quilter's Society
P. O. Box 3290 • Paducah, KY 42002-3290
www.AQSquilt.com

Located in Paducah, Kentucky, the American Quilter's Society (AQS) is dedicated to promoting the accomplishments of today's quilters. Through its publications and events, AQS strives to honor today's quiltmakers and their work and to inspire future creativity and innovation in quiltmaking.

EDITOR: BARBARA SMITH
GRAPHIC DESIGN: ELAINE WILSON
COVER DESIGN: MICHAEL BUCKINGHAM
PHOTOGRAPHY: CHARLES R. LYNCH

Library of Congress Cataloging-in-Publication Data

Poole, Linda M.
    Bended bias appliqué / by Linda M. Poole
        p. cm.
    ISBN 1-57432-853-0
    1. Appliqué--Patterns.   2. Quilting.   I. Title.

    TT779.P66   2004
    746.44'5--dc22

                                2004008262

Additional copies of this book may be ordered from the American Quilter's Society, PO Box 3290, Paducah, KY 42002-3290; 800-626-5420 (orders only please); or online at www.americanquilter.com. For all other inquiries, call 270-898-7903.

Dedication

The soul of this book was born from the strength of my parents, Gero and Gloria Grohs, who gave me love and encouragement in my childhood and adult years.

I also want to dedicate this book to the strong women friends in my life who made me believe I can follow my dreams and make a difference.

Contents

Inspiration

Where to Find Inspiration

Finding inspiration is easier than you think. Surely at some time, while in a store, you have looked at an item with a detail that has fascinated you, or perhaps you have found something exciting while you breezed through a magazine in a waiting room or while walking through a park or your own backyard.

You can easily train your mind to find inspiration in the simplest of things: gardening magazines, architectural magazines, catalogs, window boxes filled with flowers, home gardening centers, scrollwork in fences, balconies on historical homes, and design elements on monuments.

Your library is a wonderful source for design hunting. Just pick up any modern or historical art book, and you will be sure to find fascinating color blends and designs that come from your heritage.

Inspiration can be found on butterfly or dragonfly wings, with their distinctive designs. Study spider webs or dewdrops in the early morning. Sunrises and sunsets can boost your exploration to a new color palette, and icicles glisten and gleam while the sun shines through, casting fragments of colors like a rainbow.

Once I have a focus for the project I want to design, inspiration starts to pop out everywhere. Flowers seem to become abundant wherever I go, either in their natural form or as designs on billboards, cards, and labels. Bended Bias designs also follow me everywhere. Tapestries, pillows, lacework, windows, and buildings all seem to hold the details I need to encourage me.

Look at things as if you had never seen them before. The plate you eat off everyday can become quite new and refreshing once you discover its texture and design, and perhaps its shape or history. Enjoy entertaining yourself with your newly discovered talents for finding inspiration!

Bended Bias Basics

At first glance, you may think Bended Bias is just the plain old traditional bias tape we use to outline our piecing, but in reality, Bended Bias is so much grander and more stylish. Think of Bended Bias as a "designer bias tape" that softly edges and enhances your appliqué or traditional pieced blocks.

Unlike stained-glass quilts, which have bias tape around every piece, Bended Bias is an embellishment that you can add wherever you like. It is made by choosing a fabric that complements or contrasts with neighboring fabrics. For example, what if you make bias tape from a wild tiger print and use it to edge an appliquéd tiger lily? It would be really striking. In addition to using Bended Bias to edge your appliqué or pieced blocks, you can use it to emphasize open areas with scrollwork or frames.

You can use the patterns at their given size for appliqué without Bended Bias, but to add Bended Bias, you will probably want to enlarge the patterns so that you can feel comfortable using your iron to bend the tape around the shapes. For some patterns, such as the Bended Bias designs (pages 91–105), you can pre-shape the bias tape on a Teflon sheet before appliquéing it whole onto the design (see Pre-shaped Bias Designs, page 17). Bended Bias is quick and easy to make, and it is worth the extra stitches taken to make your quilts spectacular.

EGGSQUISITE COLUMBINE 29" x 23¼", detail, made by Jeanne Sullivan, Hawley, Pennsylvania. Bended Bias was used to edge the center petals of this columbine (flower pattern, page 25).

SUNSHINE, 22" x 22", detail, hand appliquéd by the author and machine quilted by Judy Irish

SHOO FLY QUILT, 49½" x 49½" (right). Pieced by the author, bias tape appliquéd by BJ Herter of Milford, Pennsylvania, and quilted by Judy Irish. Covering each seam of a pieced block with bias tape adds depth and color.

Fabrics for Bended Bias

When walking into a quilt shop, you will see every fabric color imaginable, dancing and swirling, just begging to be touched and brought home. After surviving the "Dance of the Colors" experience, stay strong, pick a fabric, unwrap a small portion of it from the bolt, and fold it on the bias (45-degree angle). The fabric design, seen as a whole on the bolt, will turn into a wonderful new design right before your eyes. Those patterns that fall so perfectly on the vertical will become fragments of color on the diagonal ... a whole new look to an otherwise common pattern.

I like to use 100 percent cotton fabric, but you are not limited to any particular type, by any means. Why do I use cotton? Well, it is familiar to me. I can predict how it will iron, fold, bend, and wash. A nice tight weave will hold up better than an inexpensive loose weave, particularly because you will be giving it a lot of "exercise" by washing, starching, ironing, folding, sewing—you get the idea.

I do highly recommend washing your fabrics first before using them. There is nothing more disappointing than to have a color bleed on a finished appliqué piece, and this recommendation comes from my own experience.

Notice how a fabric is transformed when it is made into bias tape.

Fabrics for Appliqué

After you have chosen a project to work on, you can decide on your color combinations. Would you like your appliqué to be whimsical, serious, muted, mottled, or vibrant? There is such an amazing variety of fabrics to choose from, and we are fortunate to have so many luscious colors. Perhaps a mocha java latte with a hint of espresso brown will be just the right touch for your next quilt.

Let yourself be adventurous and brave. You already know you want to appliqué, now just pick a fabric; pull anything to begin with. I call this a "jump starter" piece. You can build from it, spend hours finding fabrics to complement it, or just put it back and pick a new jump starter. Your mood will dictate your color palette, so don't fight it. Just go with the flow.

Background Fabrics

Keep in mind that the colors you have chosen for the appliqué pieces will have to be stitched to a background fabric. The background is the foundation for all the other colors that will join it. Don't let your background material compete with the appliqué colors, and make sure that your appliqué does not get lost on the background. Try to select a soft neutral color or one with hints of light swirls to enhance your appliqué.

If you are choosing a dark background, audition your appliqué pieces on top of it to be sure that you will be able to see all the appliqué details. Step back, squint your eyes, or look through a reducing lens. As long as the colors don't compete and you can see contrast, you have a winner.

Materials and Supplies

The best advice I can give is to try new tools and techniques and use what works for you. Sometimes the newest gadget isn't going to be the miracle wonder you thought it might be. Ask your friends or quilt shop staff for advice. If you're at a quilt show, watch the demonstrations and be sure to ask if you don't understand how something works. Don't be afraid to try something more than once. You may like it better the second time around. Experimentation and being open-minded will create your best chances for success.

Bias-tape makers. These tools come in several sizes for making tape in ¼" to 2" finished widths. (See page 11 for instructions on using this tool.)

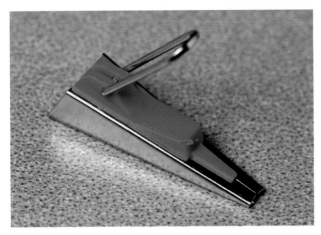

Bias-tape maker

Long shoe lace. A shoe lace is a perfect measuring tool to find the length of bias you will need for edging an appliqué piece. Simply put one end of the shoe lace down at your starting point and gently bend and walk the lace around the piece until you come to the end point. Take your shoe lace to a standard ruler to find the amount of bias tape you will need. Add an inch or so for safety,

Bodkin or tweezers. Either of these can be used to remove freezer paper from the back of a sewn appliqué piece.

Lightweight fusible tape. This product is especially good for attaching bias tape to your appliqué. You can sew through a fusible strip without gumming your needle, and it is machine washable. The iron must be set on "cotton."

Lightweight fusible interfacing. This product eliminates pinning. I like to use the lightweight fusible interfacing that can be pulled off easily when finished. I used this a lot for making circular and oval backgrounds for appliqué (see Large Appliqué Circles and Ovals, pages 18–19).

Water-soluble glue stick. Use a brand made for fabrics so it will wash out. The glue stick is used to temporarily hold two fabrics together. Remember to recap your glue stick so the glue won't dry out, and keep a damp wash cloth in a baggie to clean sticky fingers occasionally.

Teflon® Press sheet. A press sheet will protect your ironing board from fusible materials. The professional-grade sheet I use withstands 600 degrees of heat. Nothing sticks to it, and after using it, I can quickly wipe it with a damp cloth and roll it for storing.

Bended Bias Basics

Scissors. It's wise to use three pairs of scissors: one for cutting fabric, one for cutting anything other than fabric (paper, fusibles, interfacing, etc.), and a pair of 4" embroidery scissors for cutting thread, tiny seam allowances, and small pieces of fabric. Also invest in high-quality fabric scissors and embroidery scissors, which will last a lifetime. Remember to keep a sheath on the points to protect them. It's best to store your scissors in a special spot so they will not be misused for other projects.

Pins. Silk pins are thin (the thinner the better) and sharp, and they keep fabric from shifting while you work. You can keep your pins in a pin cushion filled with sand so they stay sharp at all times. I carry a little strawberry pincushion in my traveling needle and thread case.

Bias bars. These are made of plastic or metal and come in various sizes, ranging from ⅛" x 12" to ½" x 12". They are great for making very narrow bias tape. Be careful of the metal ones—they get hot.

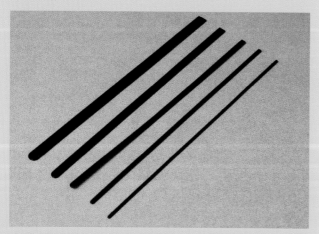

Bias bars

Bias-tape cutting ruler. On this type of ruler it is easy to see the numbers, which are shown in ¼" intervals. Slide the rotary cutter into the slot and cut perfect bias strips.

Needles. Depending on the method chosen, there are several needles to choose from. If you are hand-appliquéing Bended Bias, use a short needle to give yourself more control over your stitching. Try a size 11 or 12 hand-appliqué needle. Remember, the larger the number is on the needle packaging, the smaller the needle. Change your needles often to maintain a sharp point. Use a needle threader to help thread those tiny eyes.

Thimbles. You may need to try several thimble styles to find the one that works best for you. My preference is a clear, self-adhesive finger pad that lasts for hours.

Cutting-mat/press-board. One side is a cutting mat and the other is a cushioned press board, with a handle on top. I think these are great to bring to classes and meetings and when you're on the go.

Marking tools. Use a fine-line marking tool whose lines are easily removed with water. Use a blue water-soluble marker for best results. The lines are easily removed by dipping the finished top or quilt in cold water or spraying the marked areas with cold water. Always mark lightly and test your fabrics first to ensure the removal of the lines.

Light box or window. For tracing your patterns, you will need a light source behind the pattern. You can use a light box, or you can make a substitute by placing tempered glass between two tables with a lamp underneath the glass. My favorite method is to tape my fabric to a clean window, slip the pattern underneath, and trace.

Dressmaker's transfer paper. Using transfer paper and a tracing stylus will eliminate the need for a light box or window for tracing. You can find this specialty paper in many colors. White and yellow shows nicely on dark colors; and blue, green, and pink do well on other fabric colors.

Thread. It is important to match the thread color to the appliqué piece. A mercerized cotton embroidery thread is a good choice, and it comes in a rainbow of colors. If you cannot find a perfectly matching color, use one shade darker rather than lighter.

Other Useful Items

Iron with a pointed tip

Ironing board or surface

Rotary cutter, mat, and ruler

Compass

Yardstick compass

Lightweight cardboard

Lamp

Pointer for turning curves

Bended Bias Techniques

As quilters, we are fortunate to be able to choose whether to make our bias tape in a traditional manner or to use the gizmos and gadgets available at our quilt and fabric shops or online. If time does not permit, you can easily buy pre-made fusible tape in a wide variety of colors.

Before any bias tape can be made, the fabric needs to be washed then prepared by cutting it into strips. Start with a square piece of fabric of any convenient size. Fold it in half diagonally and iron the crease. Use a rotary cutter and ruler to cut along the crease. Then, from both pieces, cut strips the desired width as measured from the diagonal cut.

Using a Bias-Tape Maker

Bias-tape makers come in many sizes. The ¼" tape maker is suitable for Bended Bias.

1. Cut ½" fabric strips on the bias. Insert one end of a strip into the wide slot on top of the bias-tape maker. Use a pin or an awl to push the strip through the little slot (fig. 1). Then gently pull just a bit out of the other end.

2. Pin the end of the strip to the ironing board and pull the tool along the strip. Press the folded strip as you pull the tape maker (fig. 2).

Using Bias Bars

Bias bars come in plastic or metal in a variety of sizes. It is a perfect tool for making the small ⅛" bias tape. (See Making ⅛" Tape, on page 12, for another way to make this very narrow width.)

1. To use a bias bar, cut the appropriate size bias strip. (For example, to make a ¼" wide tape, cut a bias strip ¾" wide by the length needed.) Fold the strip in half around the bar, wrong sides together.

FIG. 1. Use a pin to help get the strip started.

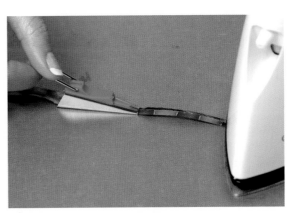

FIG. 2. Press the folded strip as it comes from the tape maker.

2. With a sewing machine zipper foot, sew (with ⅛" seam allowances) the long edges of the bias strip together, right next to the bar. (The bar should be to the left of your zipper foot.) Remove the bar and trim the seam allowances close to the stitched line with your embroidery scissors.

3. Re-insert the bar and roll the seam allowance to the center of a flat side of the bar and press. Slowly remove the bar, turn the tube over so the seam is on the bottom, and press again for a crisp crease.

When using the ⅛" or ³⁄₁₆" bias bar, dampen the fabric with a bit of water or spray starch to hold the crease.

Applying Bias Tape

1. Tear off a strip of fusible tape and press it to the underside of your bias tape. Peel off the paper. Using the tip of your iron, gently coax the Bended Bias around the appliqué piece, centering the tape on the cut edge. Be sure the bias tape strip extends ⅛" beyond the edge of the appliqué at the beginning and the end of the strip.

2. When you come to a point, place the tip of a toothpick or skewer on the point and sweep the tape around the turn (fig. 3), creating a fold. Firmly tap your iron on the point to hold the fold in place before continuing.

FIG. 3. Use a toothpick to help fold the tape at a point.

Bias tape can be added to appliqué units after the pieces have been glued but before they have been appliquéd together. Decide where you would like to add your Bended Bias and either add a light fusible tape to the back of the bias tape then iron the tape onto the unit, or dab a little glue stick on the back of the tape and position it with your fingers. Appliqué the pieces and bias tape together to complete the unit.

Stitching Bended Bias

For machine sewing Bended Bias, an open-toed embroidery foot will allow you to see your work easily. Use an awl or a stiletto to help guide the bias tape through the machine and keep the fabric and tape from puckering.

Experiment with machine or hand embroidery stitches for sewing your bias tapes. You can find a number of books that contain a multitude of interesting stitches to enhance your work. I like to use these stitches: blind hem, top stitch, blanket, twin needle, and some decorative stitches. Check your sewing machine manual to find the appropriate needle size and stitch length for each one.

Making ⅛" Bias Tape

Want to make teeny tiny baby bias? It's easier than you think. With your bias-tape maker, make the traditional ¼" bias tape. Once it has cooled and the crease has been set, run your glue stick along the seam. Fold the tape in half.

The resulting bias tape may be thick, but it will add dimension to your work. Stitch it down the same way you would the wider bias tape.

If you want the Bended Bias to shine alone on your appliqué, then you can hand appliqué the bias tape, or you can machine sew it with monofilament thread, which is invisible.

To add some sparkle to your piece, you can add different embellishments, like sequins, shiny beads, or French knots.

Appliqué Techniques

Glue-stick appliqué, which is a turned-edge method, is described here, and a raw-edged fused method, The Teflon Technique, is described on page 16, but you can use any appliqué method you like.

Glue-Stick Appliqué

For glue-stick appliqué, you need to have the following supplies on hand:

Background fabric
Fabric for appliqué pieces
Matching thread
Appliqué needles
Freezer paper
Pencil
Light box (optional)
Transfer paper and tracing stylus (optional)
Water-soluble blue marker
Paper and fabric scissors
Water-soluble glue stick
Skewer or toothpick
Bodkin or tweezers
Iron and ironing surface
Small piece of lightweight cardboard
Warm water
Damp wash cloth
Towel

Making a Master Copy

Note that asymmetrical patterns are reversed relative to the quilts in the photos, so that the appliqué templates will be reversed. These reversed templates, when traced on the wrong side of the fabrics, produce the correct orientation in the finished quilt.

1. Use a photocopier to enlarge your chosen pattern to the size you want, or if you are content with the size provided, you can trace the pattern by hand on the dull side of a sheet of freezer paper. The appliqué pieces are numbered in the order they are to be sewn to the background. Transfer the numbers to the master copy (fig. 4).

Bias stems and bias-tape areas do not need to be labeled, but you will want to trace them on the master copy and the background to use as placement guides.

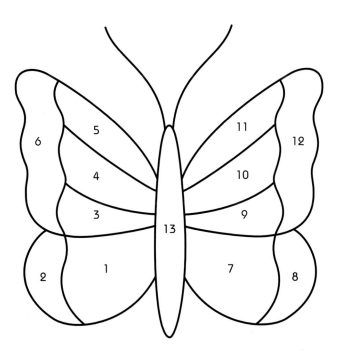

FIG. 4. Be sure to add the appliqué numbers to the master copy.

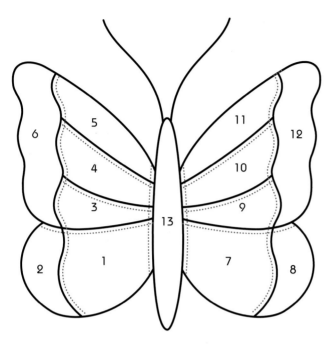

FIG. 5. Place dots along the edges that don't need to be turned under.

Using Dressmaker's Transfer Paper

Instead of using a light source to transfer a pattern to the background fabric, you can use dressmaker's transfer paper.

1. Tape the background fabric, right side up on a table and tape the colored side of the transfer paper face down on the background.

2. Tape your master pattern, face down, over the transfer paper. You should be able to see the pattern, oriented as in the quilt photo, through the master copy.

3. With the tracing stylus held vertically, apply pressure to retrace the pattern. Periodically, take a careful peek at your tracing to make sure you are applying enough pressure.

2. To make a template copy, tape the master, shiny side down, to a window or light box. Tape another piece of freezer paper, also shiny side down, over your master copy.

3. With a pencil or a thin permanent marker, retrace the entire pattern on the dull side of the second sheet of freezer paper. Include the appliqué numbers. This copy will be cut apart to make your appliqué templates.

Overlapping Pieces

1. Look at each flower or design to determine where pieces overlap. A "closed" area is one that must have the seam allowances turned under before being appliquéd. An "open" area does not need to be turned because it will be covered by another piece.

2. On the template pattern, indicate the open areas on each piece by making little dots along the edge. Just think of the dots as little "o's" for the word "open" (see fig. 5).

3. With your paper scissors, cut the template pattern pieces apart on the drawn lines.

Cutting Fabric Pieces

1. Place the freezer-paper templates shiny side down on the wrong side of the appropriate fabrics and press them for a few seconds with a dry, medium iron (fig. 6). Check to make sure that the freezer paper has adhered to the fabric.

2. When you cut the fabric pieces, add a ³⁄₁₆" turn-under allowance around the templates. There really is no need to measure exactly, just add the seam allowances by eye.

3. Stopping short of the turn line, clip the inside curves of the closed sections with your small embroidery scissors (fig. 7).

Turning Allowances

1. Use a piece of cardboard to keep your table surface clean when using a glue stick. With the appliqué piece wrong side up, lightly spread glue on the allowances along the closed sections.

2. Turn the allowances under and use a damp washcloth to wipe your fingers clean of any glue residue.

Making Units

1. Decide which pieces need to be joined as a unit before being appliquéd to the background. For each unit, lightly spread glue on the wrong side of the allowances in the appropriate open sections.

2. Hold the pieces up to a window, lamp, or light box to help in positioning them and use your fingers to press the overlapping pieces together. Then appliqué the pieces. Continue adding pieces in this manner until the unit is complete (fig. 8).

Preparing the Background

1. Cut a piece of background fabric an inch or two larger than the size needed for your quilt project.

2. Tape your master copy, pattern side down, to a light box or window. With the master right side down, the image will match the orientation of the design in the quilt.

3. Center the background fabric, right side up, on the pattern. Tape the fabric to the light box or window and, with a thin water-soluble blue marker, lightly trace the pattern on the fabric. This tracing is a placement guide for the appliquéd units, so you need not mark every single detail.

4. Using the traced lines on the background fabric for reference, appliqué your units to the background.

FIG. 6. Press freezer-paper templates on the wrong side of fabrics.

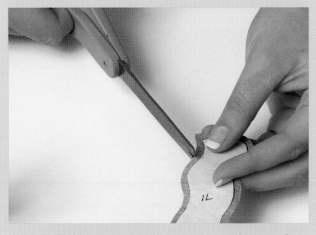

FIG. 7. Clip the seam allowances on the inside curves for those areas that will be turned under.

FIG. 8. Appliqué pieces into units before attaching them to the background.

PATRIOTIC STARS sample. These stars were made with the Teflon Technique.

Removing Freezer Paper

1. After the final appliqué has been sewn, soak the entire piece in lukewarm water and agitate slowly with your hand or, using a bucket of water and a clean sponge, slowly dab the piece in sections to loosen the freezer paper.

2. Gently remove the loosened freezer paper with a bodkin or tweezers.

3. Dip the piece in clean water, then gently squeeze the excess water out by hand. Roll the piece in a thick towel to remove more water.

4. Gently steam press the appliqué on a clean dry towel.

The Teflon Technique

For this raw-edge fused method, you will need the following supplies:

Lightweight fusible web
Lightweight fusible tape
Masking tape or blue painter's tape
Lightweight cardboard
Glue stick or spray glue
Background fabric
Fabric for appliqué pieces
Matching thread
Appliqué needles or sewing machine
Pencil
Paper and fabric scissors
Skewer or toothpick
See-through Teflon press sheet
Bodkin or tweezers
Iron and ironing surface

This method eliminates the need for appliquéing each individual fabric piece to the background before adding the bias tape.

1. Enlarge your chosen pattern to the size you need for your project. Be sure to transfer the appliqué numbers to this master copy.

2. Place fusible web, paper side up, over the master copy and use a pencil to trace the pattern on the fusible, including the appliqué numbers.

3. Using paper scissors, cut the pieces from the fusible web and sort them by number.

4. Iron the web pieces, textured side down, on the backs of the appropriate fabrics. Use fabric scissors to cut the fabric pieces, on the line, and sort them by number.

5. Tape the master copy, right side down, on a Teflon sheet, then turn the sheet over. The pattern will be visible through the sheet.

6. Select piece 1, remove the paper, and fuse it in place on the background. Continue fusing pieces in numerical order until you come to one you want to outline with bias tape. Outline that piece, then continue adding appliqué and bias tape to complete the design.

7. Press the whole piece and set it aside to cool. Lift up the entire unit and fuse it to the background. Machine or hand appliqué the bias tape to the background, which should catch the raw edges of the appliqué pieces.

Pre-shaped Bias Designs

For some patterns, bias tape can be completely shaped before being appliquéd to the background (see the Bended Bias patterns and the frame patterns, on pages 91–105).

1. Enlarge your chosen pattern to the size you need. Tape the master copy, right side down, on a Teflon sheet, then turn the sheet over. The pattern will be visible through the sheet.

2. Tear off a strip of fusible tape and press it to the underside of your bias tape. Peel off the paper. Using the tip of your iron, gently coax the Bended Bias around the design.

3. When the design has been completely outlined with bias tape, press the fused unit as a whole, then leave it on the Teflon sheet to cool (fig. 9). Pick up the entire piece as a unit, place it on your background, and iron it in place.

4. Machine or hand appliqué the bias tape unit to the background. If you machine sew it in place, using a twin needle creates an interesting look. A different effect can be achieved by sewing the edges with a tiny contrasting blanket stitch.

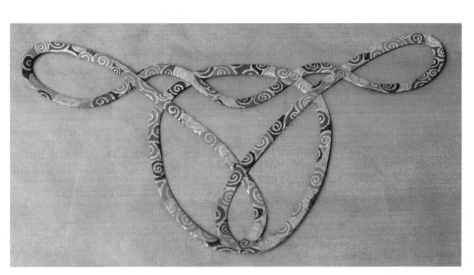

FIG. 9. Bias tape design created on a Teflon press sheet

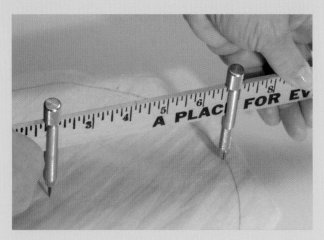

FIG. 10. Yardstick compass

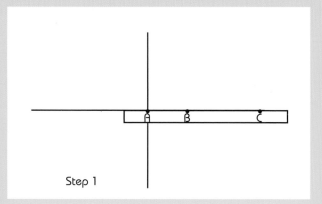

Step 1

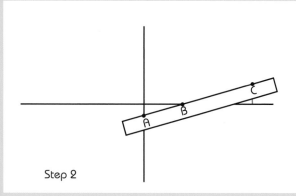

Step 2

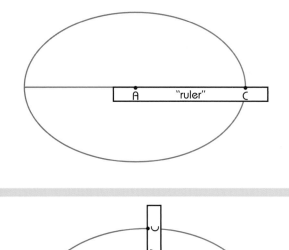

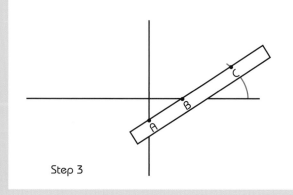

Step 3

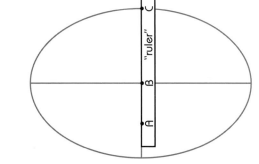

FIG. 11. A to C is half the oval's desired length. B to C is half the oval's width.

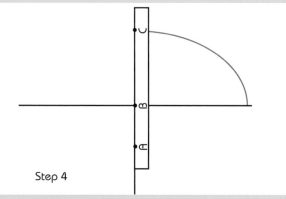

Step 4

FIG. 12. Steps to drawing an oval of any size

Large Appliqué Circles and Ovals

Instead of setting your appliqué work inside a traditional square, try an oval or circle for something a little different. Once you master the method, and believe me, it's very easy to learn, you may get hooked.

Drawing Large Circles

1. Use a yardstick compass to draw a circle in the size needed on a piece of cardboard to make a traditional template, or you can draw the circle on the paper side of a lightweight fusible interfacing (fig. 10).

2. Cut the circle, leaving about a ½" seam allowance beyond the drawn line, or slightly more to be on the safe side.

3. The interfacing has a slightly bumpy surface that goes face down on the appliqué block, which is face up. Center the drawn circle on the appliqué block and press it gently, lightly, and quickly to just tack it in place.

4. Sew completely around the circle on the pencil line, and trim the seam allowance to ¼".

5. Cut a slit into the interfacing, not quite to the seam line, and turn the piece right side out. Use a pointer or another tool with a rounded end to slide into the slit to smooth out the seam. Appliqué your circle on a background fabric.

Drawing Large Ovals

1. Drawing large ovals is easier than you might imagine. First, decide how long and wide you want your oval to be. Cut a strip of lightweight cardboard or template plastic that is an inch or two longer than half the oval's length and about 1" wide. This strip will become your "ruler."

2. Referring to figure 11, mark an A near the left end of your ruler. Then add B and C as follows: The distance between A and C is half the length of the desired oval. The distance between B and C is half its width.

3. In the middle of a piece of paper, large enough to accommodate the oval, draw a line the length of the desired oval. At the center of the line, draw another line perpendicular to the first one for the oval's width.

4. Align your ruler as shown in Step 1 of figure 12 and place a mark on the paper at C. Move the A mark a short way down the vertical line and adjust B along the horizontal line. Make another mark at C. Keeping A on the vertical line and B on the horizontal line, continue moving the ruler short distances and marking the oval at C.

5. When A, B, and C are aligned on the vertical line, you will have marked one fourth of the oval. Repeat the marking instructions for each quarter to complete the oval.

Alternatively, an oval can be made by folding a sheet of paper into quarters and using your ruler to draw one quarter of the oval on the folded sheet (fig. 13). Cut the folded paper on the line. Unfold the paper to reveal the completed oval.

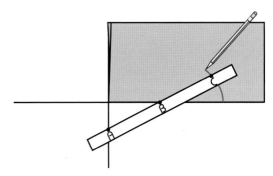

FIG. 13. Mark a quarter of the oval on a piece of paper folded in fourths.

Ideas for Quilting

Judy Irish, who owns and operates Wild Irish Rows in Arlington, Washington, has quilted many of my sample quilts. When I asked her about machine quilting, Judy told me, *"It is really no mystery. You must be willing to practice, throw caution to the wind ... and have FUN. Do not be hampered by rules, preconceived notions, or how you think things should look, and most of all, quilt for yourself and not for others."*

With all of that said, you must know that she buys quilting and design books nearly by the carload. Judy especially looks for books with new and different techniques, which not only inspire her creative side and help with technical skills, but also plant seeds for new designs to add to her doodling sketch book (fig. 14).

For you, too, one of the best ways to improve your machine quilting is to keep a journal of doodles or sketches. Whenever you see something that sparks your interest, sketch it down quickly or photograph it. It can be an interesting piece of architecture, a beautiful leaf, a floor tile, carpet design, fabric pattern, or countless other things you pass by every day.

Tips from Judy Irish

Quilter Judy Irish offers these practical tips to make your quilting life much easier:

Choose your backing fabric carefully. A busy middle value will be great to hide imperfect stitching, especially for beginners. If using a plain or muslin back, the fewer the thread color changes the better. One thread color is usually best, or choose a fabric that will best go with your thread changes or bobbin thread color.

Marking your quilts can be done with chalk, pounce pads, marking pencils, or blue water soluble pens, but my personal favorite is no marking! I practice so I can do my quilting without a pattern, and you can

do it too ... just practice, practice, practice. There is something magical about repeating a design on paper, over and over. Repetition is the key.

If you do need a little guide, you can draw or trace a bird or bug or whatever on tracing paper, freezer paper, or plain white paper; cut out the shape; and spray adhesive on the back of the paper cutout. Then stick the cutout on the quilt and simply sew around the edge. When you remove the paper, you can fill in with free-hand squiggles.

The secret to pin basting the quilt layers is to use zillions of pins. If you place your hand, palm open, on the quilt, you need to have several pins under your hand. This is the best protection against puckers.

If you want to avoid pinning, take advantage of an adhesive spray baste, which makes life much simpler. Just follow the directions on the can.

When setting up your sewing area, be sure you can reach your machine easily, and sit comfortably relaxed so you don't get a stiff neck. Play music, relax your neck and shoulders, and have fun. Once you realize you are not performing brain surgery, you will be on your way to a truly original quilting design.

I use Metallica needles in my machine for quilting, and in fact, I use them for piecing as well. That way, I never have to try to figure out which needle is in the machine, and I can change threads without a second thought.

For variegated threads, I use a middle value to make the blending work better. Another tip is to match the bobbin thread to the background of the quilt top. This will help keep the little "pokies" of bobbin thread from popping up to the top of the quilt.

Don't be afraid to play with your thread tension, including the bobbin thread ... righty tighty, lefty loosie! I change my thread tensions whenever I have to in order to have thread look its best on the top and the bottom. You can always put the tension back where it was.

When quilting, I usually just grab the quilt sandwich with my hands and guide it wherever I want to go. I don't use bicycle clips, gloves, or other aids for machine quilting. My grab system works well for a quilt of any size.

One of my favorite quilting techniques for appliqué quilts is to stitch the background with flowers and stems that echo the appliquéd flowers. This is a great way to fill up the space with creative stitching rather than using a meander or echo stitch.

It is always a good idea to make some practice sandwiches with the batting, thread, and fabric of the quilt you want to do. That way you can get the bugs out before you work on the real thing.

It's also a good idea to start with baby, charity, and college quilts ... save the one for the big show until you have a few other quilts under your belt.

Keep your sense of humor, have realistic expectations, and remember that we always see our mistakes as big as the Grand Canyon. Chances are no one else will take notice at all.

By the way, I really do not like to use the word mistake, so we can eliminate that whole word from our vocabulary.

Take time to get a little perspective on your work. This is only a quilt. Nothing can really hurt it, and if all else fails, you can make another one. It is not as if we are running out of fabric!

The only mystery to me about machine quilting is why people think it is so difficult. I promise that, if you try to quilt on your own, using proper equipment and plenty of practice, you will soon be a pro and have a lot of fun in the process. Just throw away those rules you thought you had to obey, and follow your needle and your heart instead.

Fig. 14. Quilting doodles, by longarm quilter Judy Irish

More quilting doodles by longarm quilter Judy Irish

Bended Bias Patterns

For appliqué without Bended Bias, you can use the following patterns at the size given or enlarge them to suit your needs.

To add Bended Bias, it's a good idea to enlarge the patterns to make the bias tape easier to handle around curves. A suggested enlargement, based on a 15" block, is given with each pattern.

A LITTLE SWIRL OF LIME, 27½" x 30", by Susan Gerhardt, South Thomaston, Maine

Columbine

Eggsquisite Columbine
29" x 23¼", made by Jeanne Sullivan of Hawley, Pennsylvania. About this pattern, the author says, "Columbine grows wild where I live, and it was a natural choice to add this flower to my bouquet. Just a hint of bias tape on the opened flower is enough to show the columbine off."

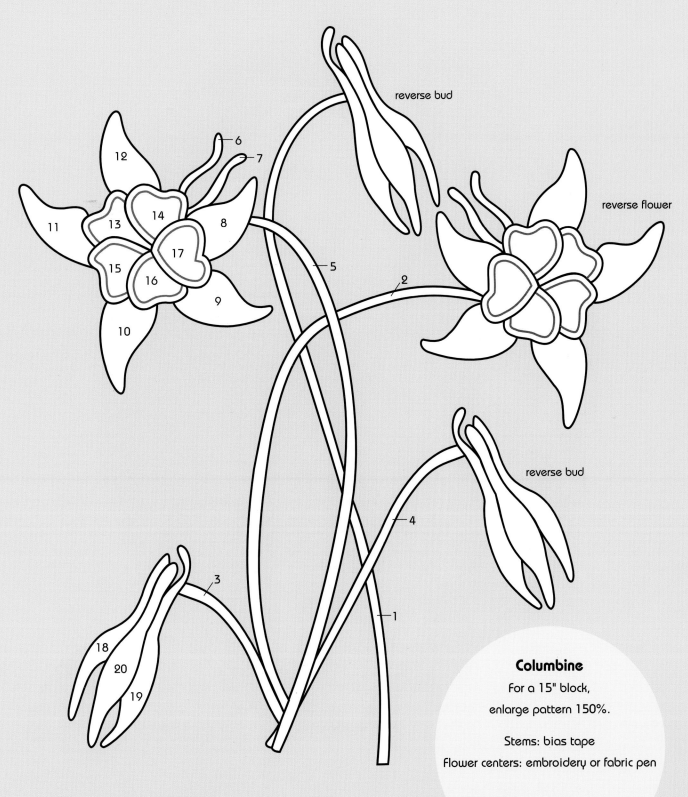

reverse bud

reverse flower

reverse bud

6
7
12
11
13
14
17
8
15
16
9
10
5
2
4
1
3
18
20
19

Columbine

For a 15" block,
enlarge pattern 150%.

Stems: bias tape
Flower centers: embroidery or fabric pen

Bended Bias: gray lines indicate
suggested placement.

Wild Rose

WILD ROSE

19¾" x 23¾", detail, hand appliquéd by the author and quilted by Judy Irish. Two ovals were used to achieve this crescent moon effect. A cluster of beads was sewn to the flower center, and longer beads were used to create a circle around the center.

Wild Rose

For a 15" block,
enlarge pattern 150%.

Stems: bias tape
Flower center: beads

Bended Bias: gray lines indicate
suggested placement.

Anemone

CAMEO FLOWERS
53" x 51", detail, made by the author and her mother, Gloria Grohs, of Milford, Pennsylvania. For the anemone, choose colors in different shades to help distinguish the petals.

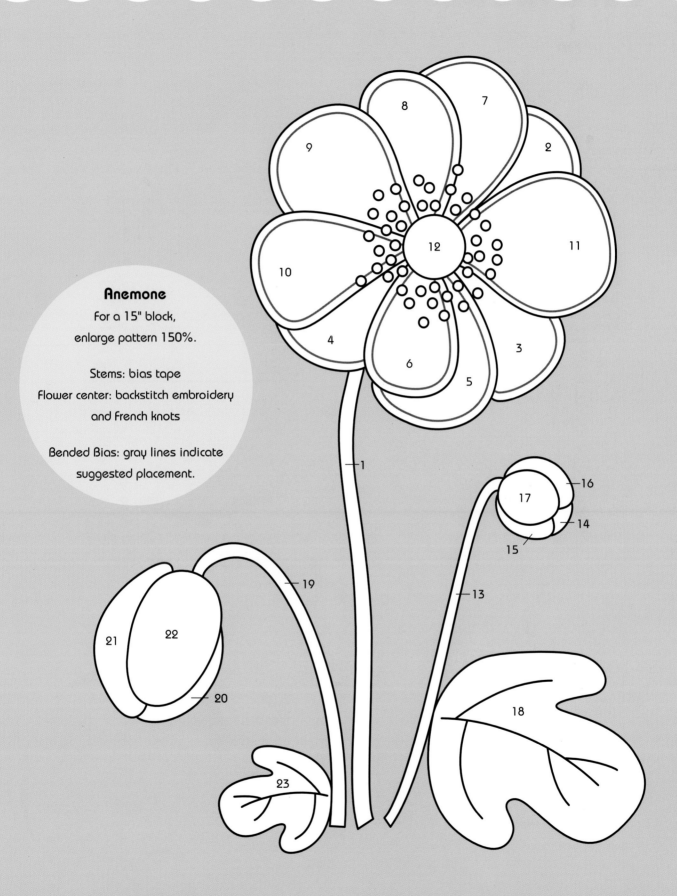

Anemone

For a 15" block,
enlarge pattern 150%.

Stems: bias tape
Flower center: backstitch embroidery
and French knots

Bended Bias: gray lines indicate
suggested placement.

Hibiscus

CAMEO FLOWERS
53" x 51", detail, made by the author and her mother, Gloria Grohs, of Milford, Pennsylvania. The hibiscus fabric was hand painted with acid-free, non-toxic, dual-colored markers after the appliqué was completed.

Hibiscus

For a 15" block,
enlarge pattern 150%.

Stems: bias tape
Flower center: backstitch embroidery
and French knots

Bended Bias: gray lines indicate
suggested placement.

Pansy

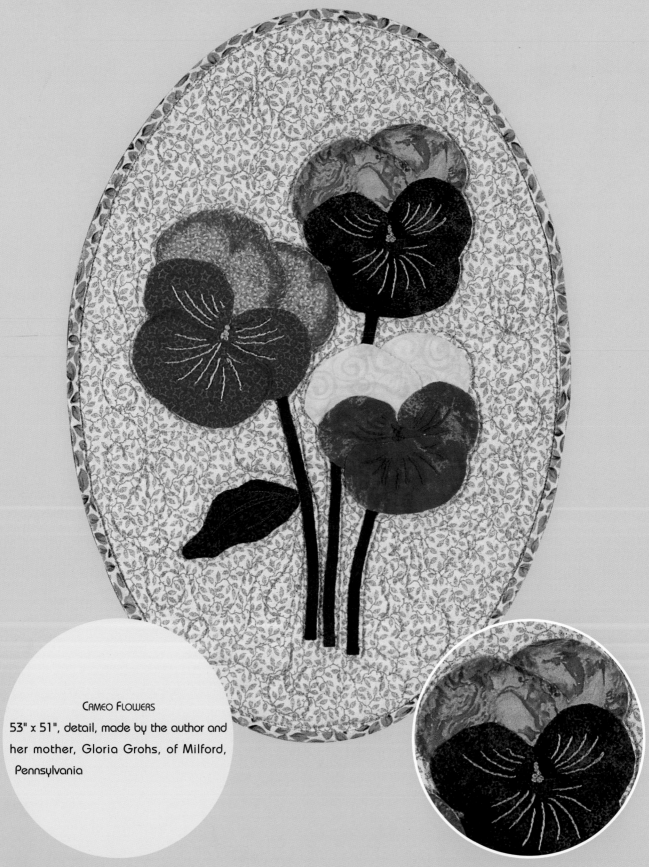

CAMEO FLOWERS
53" x 51", detail, made by the author and her mother, Gloria Grohs, of Milford, Pennsylvania

Bended Bias APPLIQUÉ ~ Linda M. Poole

Pansy

For a 15" block,
enlarge pattern 150%.

Stems: bias tape
Flower petals and leaf veins: embroidery
Flower center: beads or
French knots

Bended Bias: gray lines indicate
suggested placement.

Day Lily

TROPICAL LILY

42" x 42½", made by Laura Orben of Milford, Pennsylvania. A contrasting Bended Bias tape gives a tropical feel to this lily. To add a bias tape border to an oval, fold the oval into equal sections. Place a component of the bias pattern on each fold, then stretch the design connections to meet each component. Making ovals is described on page 19. Pattern used to create the bias tape border, page 92.

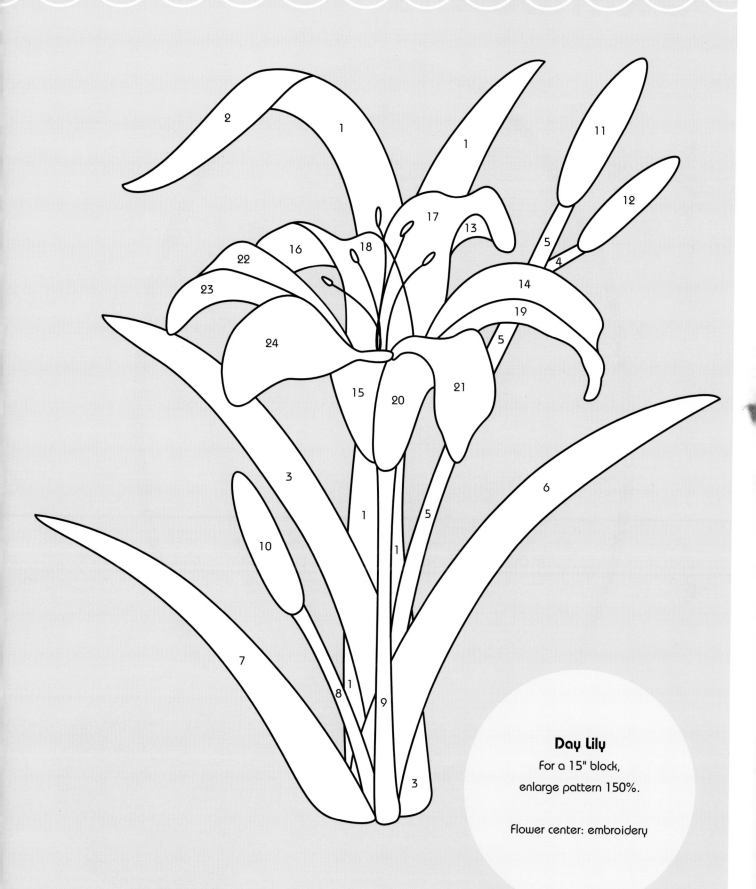

Day Lily

For a 15" block,
enlarge pattern 150%.

Flower center: embroidery

Starflowers

STARFLOWERS

26" x 30¾", detail, hand appliquéd by the author and machine quilted by Judy Irish

Bended Bias APPLIQUÉ ~ Linda M. Poole

Daisies

For a 15" block,
enlarge pattern 150%.

Stems: bias tape

Bended Bias: gray lines indicate
suggested placement.

Tulips

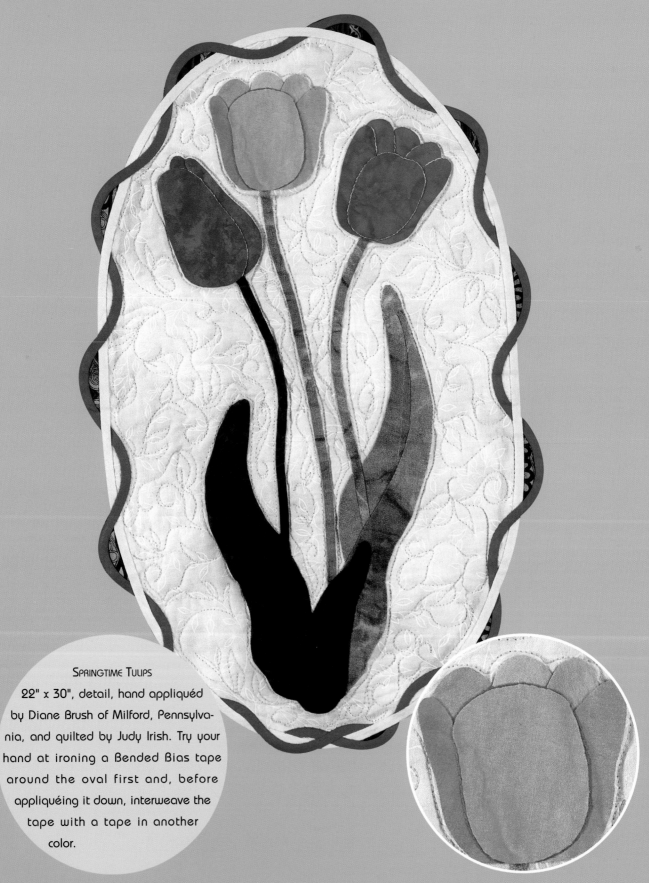

SPRINGTIME TULIPS
22" x 30", detail, hand appliquéd by Diane Brush of Milford, Pennsylvania, and quilted by Judy Irish. Try your hand at ironing a Bended Bias tape around the oval first and, before appliquéing it down, interweave the tape with a tape in another color.

Bended Bias APPLIQUÉ ~ Linda M. Poole

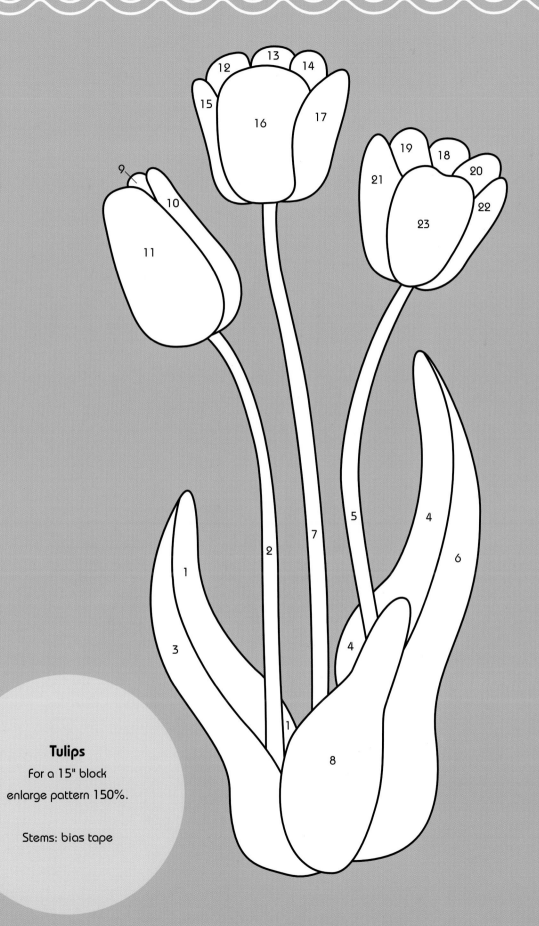

Tulips

For a 15" block
enlarge pattern 150%.

Stems: bias tape

Wine Cup

Wine Cup
24½" x 27¼", detail, made by the author. Looking at the small buds, you can see that the fabric was selectively cut to show little speckles of dots at the bottom of each segment.

Wine Cup
For a 15" block
enlarge pattern 150%.

Stems: bias tape
Flower centers and leaf veins:
embroidery

Bended Bias: gray lines indicate
suggested placement.

Calla Lilies

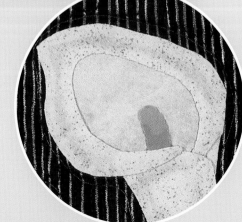

CALLA LILY

21½" x 22¾", detail, hand appliquéd
by the author and quilted by Judy Irish.
The ⅛" Bended Bias scallops, made from
the same print as the borders, add a
great deal of pleasure and interest
to this simple quilt.

Bended Bias APPLIQUÉ ~ Linda M. Poole

Calla Lilies

For a 15" block
enlarge pattern 150%.

Stems: bias tape

Bended Bias: gray lines indicate
suggested placement.

Rose

AMALIA'S BOUQUET
50" x 53", detail, made by Amalia
Emmie Lyle of Lackawaxen, Pennsylvania.
Amalia, who shares her mother's name,
used flowers from both of their weddings
in creating this bouquet.

Bended Bias APPLIQUÉ ~ Linda M. Poole

Rose

For a 15" block
pattern is 100%.

Stem: bias tape
Rose Buds patterns, pages 48–49.

Bended Bias: gray lines indicate
suggested placement.

Rose Buds

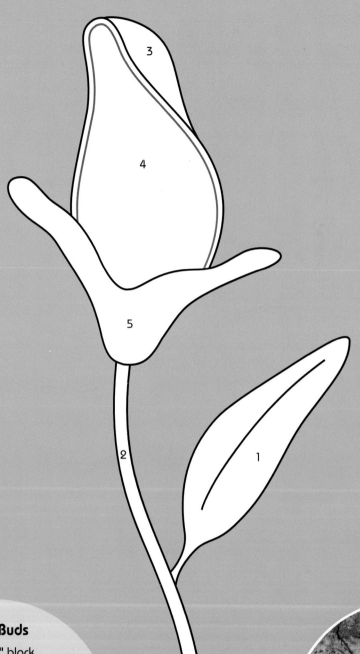

3

4

5

2

1

Rose Buds

For a 15" block
pattern is 100%.

Stems: bias tape
Quilt detail photo, page 46

Bended Bias: gray lines indicate
suggested placement.

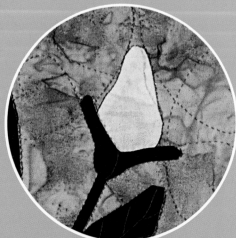

48

Bended Bias APPLIQUÉ ~ Linda M. Poole

Rose Buds

For a 15" block
pattern is 100%.

Stems: bias tape
Quilt detail photo, page 46

Bended Bias: gray lines indicate
suggested placement.

Snowdrops

SNOWDROPS IN SPRINGTIME

34½" x 34", hand appliquéd by the author and quilted by Judy Irish. Using bias scrollwork in light blue and white gives this quilt a little winter-spring enchantment. Bias tape scrollwork pattern, page 104.

Snowdrops

For a 15" block
enlarge pattern 150%.

Stems: bias tape

Daffodils & Crocus

HERALDS OF SPRING

46½" x 45", made by Helen Umstead, Lords Valley, Pennsylvania. The petals of the daffodils and crocuses were subtly enhanced by backstitch embroidery. Bias tape border pattern, page 100. Crocus pattern, page 55.

Bended Bias APPLIQUÉ ~ Linda M. Poole

Daffodils

For a 15" block
enlarge pattern 150%.

Stems: bias tape
Flower leaves and petals: backstitch
embroidery
Flower centers: beads
Bended Bias: gray lines indicate
suggested placement.

Daffodils & Crocus

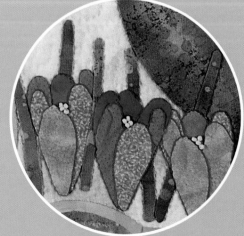

HERALDS OF SPRING
46½" x 45", detail, made by Helen
Umstead, Lords Valley, Pennsylvania.
Daffodils pattern, page 53.

Bended Bias APPLIQUÉ ~ Linda M. Poole

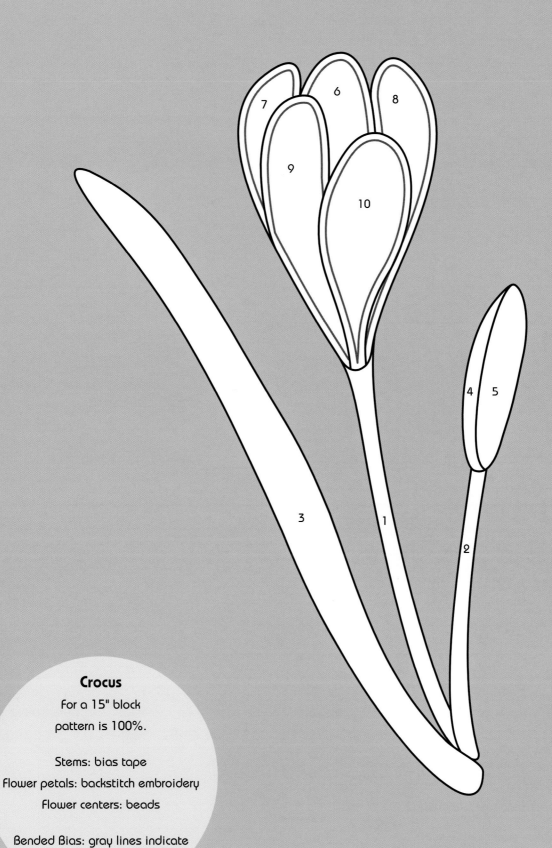

Crocus

For a 15" block
pattern is 100%.

Stems: bias tape
Flower petals: backstitch embroidery
Flower centers: beads

Bended Bias: gray lines indicate
suggested placement.

Water Lily

THE LILY POND

39" x 27½", hand appliquéd by the author and quilted by Judy Irish. To add an element of interest, reverse one of the flower designs. Bended Bias was used to show the gentle rhythm of flowing water.

Bended Bias **APPLIQUÉ** ~ Linda M. Poole

Water Lily

For a 15" block
enlarge pattern 150%.

Bended Bias: gray lines indicate
suggested placement.

Fuchsias

Bended Bias APPLIQUÉ ~ Linda M. Poole

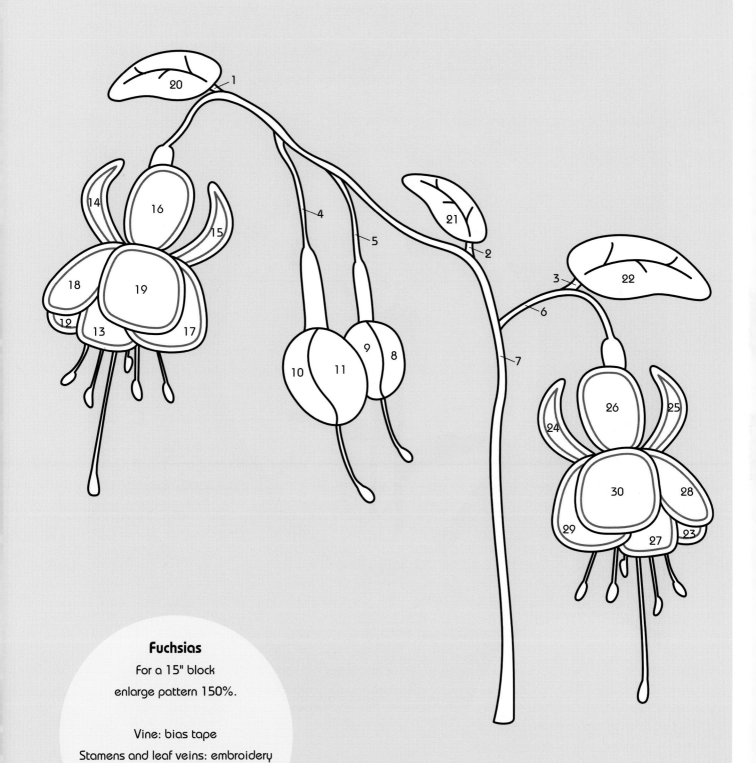

Fuchsias

For a 15" block
enlarge pattern 150%.

Vine: bias tape
Stamens and leaf veins: embroidery

Bended Bias: gray lines indicate
suggested placement.

Coneflowers

PICTURE PERFECT POSIES
22¾" x 26¾", made by Kathy J. Isaacks of Matamoras, Pennsylvania. For a variation, you can use beads or French knots in place of the appliquéd center cones. The frame around the flowers is made from ½" Bended Bias.

Bended Bias APPLIQUÉ ~ Linda M. Poole

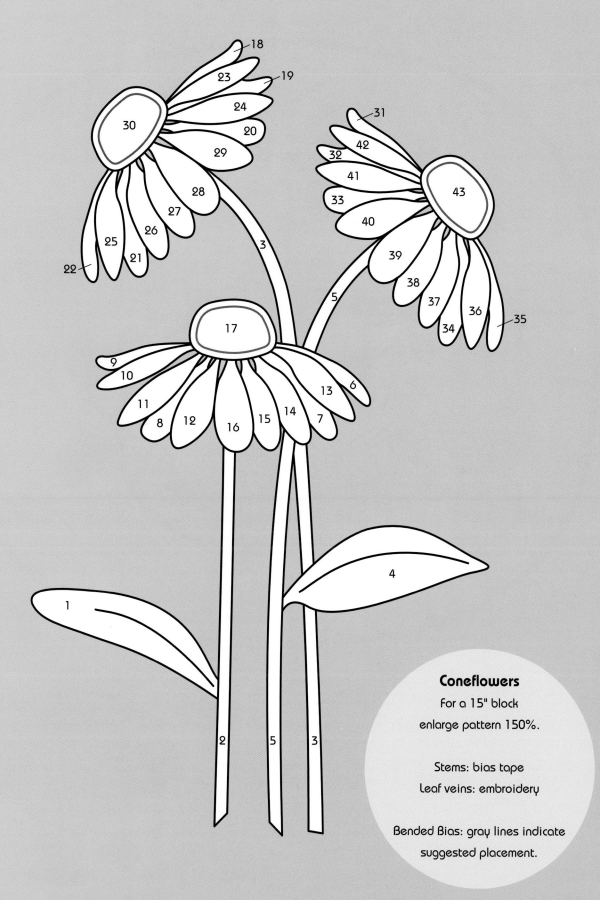

Coneflowers

For a 15" block
enlarge pattern 150%.

Stems: bias tape
Leaf veins: embroidery

Bended Bias: gray lines indicate
suggested placement.

Morning Glory

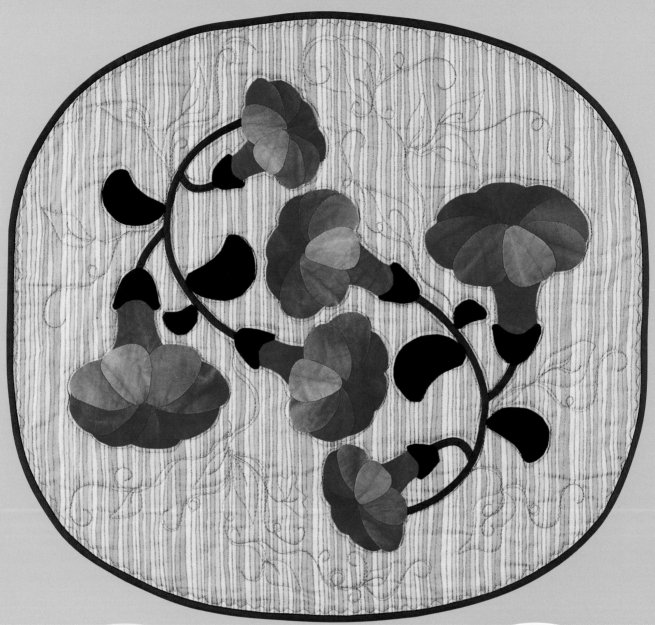

MORNING GLORIA

37" x 35", detail, made by Gloria Grohs, Milford, Pennsylvania. I could not resist naming this appliquéd flower "Morning Gloria" after my mom, Gloria, who hand appliquéd this beauty. Note that the pattern is repeated, and the two pieces are fitted together to make one larger piece.

Morning Glory

For a 15" block
enlarge pattern 150%.

Stems: bias tape

Bended Bias: gray lines indicate
suggested placement.

Chinese Lanterns

PAPER LANTERNS

16¼" x 10¾", detail, made by the author. The lanterns are set on a background circle with two sides cut off. The resulting shape is edged in maroon bias tape.

Bended Bias APPLIQUÉ ~ Linda M. Poole

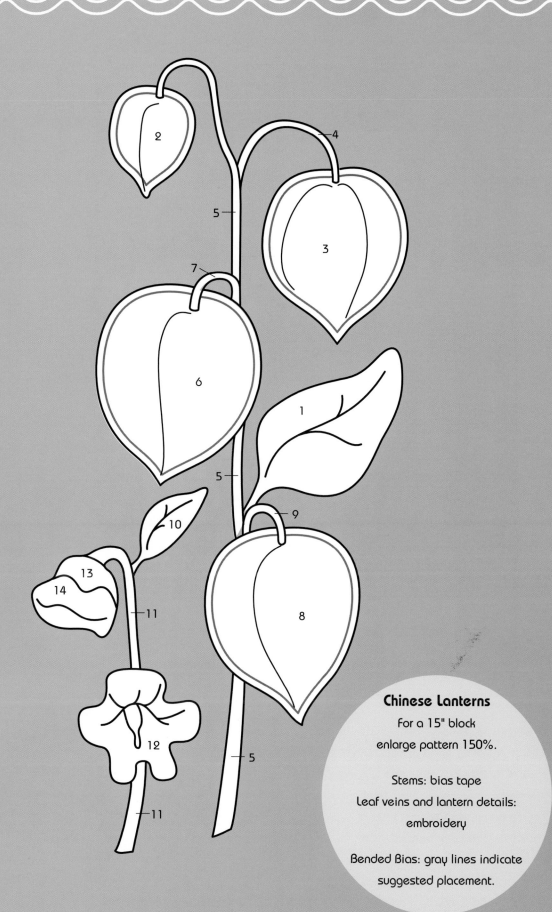

Chinese Lanterns

For a 15" block
enlarge pattern 150%.

Stems: bias tape
Leaf veins and lantern details:
embroidery

Bended Bias: gray lines indicate
suggested placement.

Tiger Lilies

A TIGER'S TAIL
21¼" x 24½", hand appliquéd and machine quilted by Carol A. Hill of Milford, Pennsylvania. Carol used the Tiger Lily pattern to add interest to two of the corners of this Bended Bias pattern, page 94.

Bended Bias APPLIQUÉ ~ Linda M. Poole

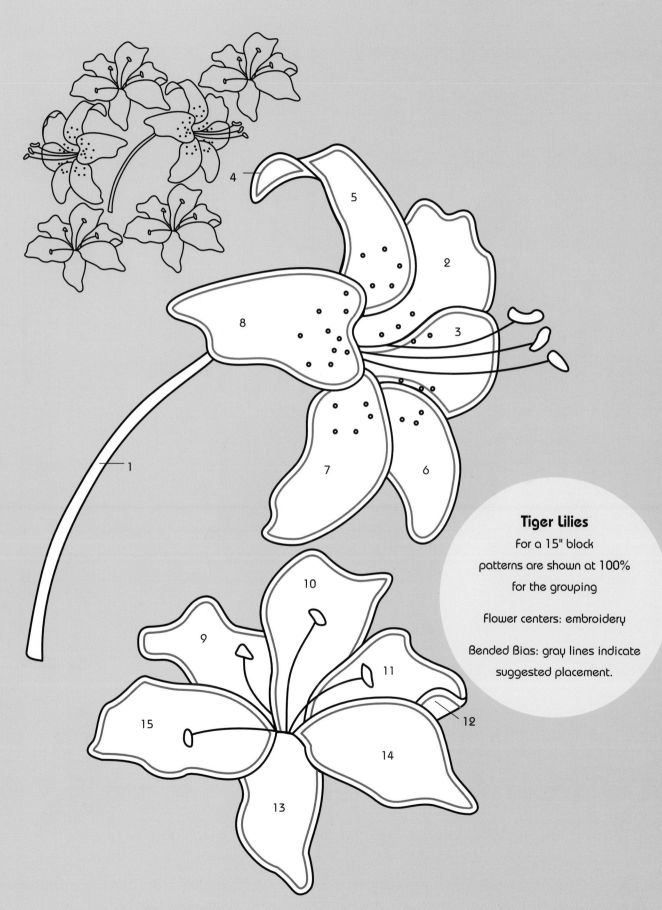

Tiger Lilies

For a 15" block
patterns are shown at 100%
for the grouping

Flower centers: embroidery

Bended Bias: gray lines indicate
suggested placement.

Impatiens

BURSTING BLOOMS
18¼" x 18¼", made by the author.
Have fun giving your quilts a new look
by setting your appliqué in different
shapes.

Impatiens

For a 15" block
enlarge pattern 150%.

Flower centers: beads
Leaf veins: embroidery

Bended Bias: gray lines indicate
suggested placement.

Flowered Heart

TRIPLE HEARTS

35" x 35¼", hand appliquéd by the author and machine quilted by Judy Irish. In this piece, the petals, leaves, and bias tape were appliquéd to light blue fabric. The outside portion of the blue fabric was then cut away next to the heart shape. Three of these heart shapes were appliquéd to a red circle before the circle was appliquéd to the hand-dyed background.

Flowered Heart

For a 15" block
enlarge pattern 150%.

Bended Bias: gray lines indicate
suggested placement.

Sunshine Butterflies

Sunshine Butterflies

For a 15" block
enlarge pattern 150%.

Antennae: embroidery or fabric pen

Bended Bias: gray lines indicate
suggested placement.

Fly Away Home Butterflies

Fly Away Home
29" x 23", machine appliquéd and quilted by Bonnie Boehm of Greeley, Pennsylvania. You can make butterfly "families" by enlarging the patterns to different sizes. Enjoy adding beads, sequins, glittery threads, rhinestones, and whatever else you can think of.

Bended Bias APPLIQUÉ ~ Linda M. Poole

Fly Away Home Butterflies

For a 15" block
enlarge pattern 150%.

Antennae: embroidery or fabric pen

Bended Bias: gray lines indicate
suggested placement.

I Spy Butterflies

I Spy Butterflies
52" x 78", made by the author. I used different applications of designer bias tape and embellishments.

I Spy Butterflies

For a 15" block
enlarge pattern 150%.

Antennae: embroidery or fabric pen

Bended Bias: gray lines indicate
suggested placement.

Dragonfly

Bended Bias APPLIQUÉ ~ Linda M. Poole

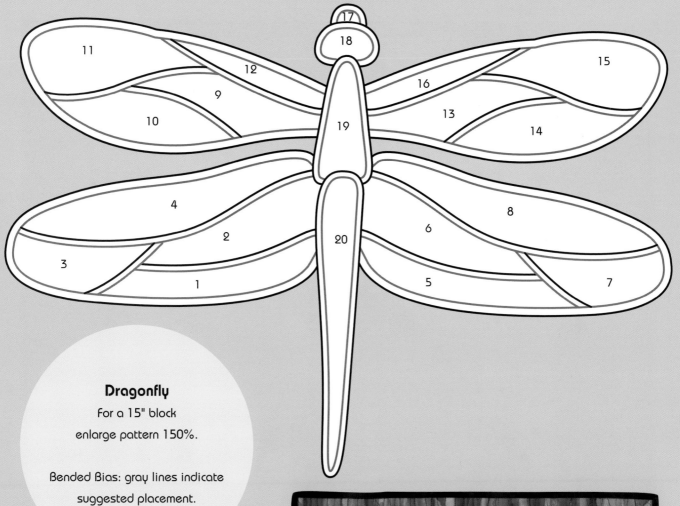

17
18
11
12
16
9
15
10
13
19
14
4
8
2
6
3
20
1
5
7

Dragonfly

For a 15" block
enlarge pattern 150%.

Bended Bias: gray lines indicate
suggested placement.

DRAGONFLY
22" x 22", detail, made by the author. The
veins in the wings are hand embroidered.

Hummingbirds

HUMMINGBIRD AND HIBISCUS
52" x 56", made by JoAnne Finnegan of Dingmans Ferry, Pennsylvania. For whatever flower you choose, you can rotate, flip, and maneuver your birds to your liking. Hummingbird patterns, pages 81–83; Hibiscus pattern, page 30.

Bended Bias APPLIQUÉ ~ Linda M. Poole

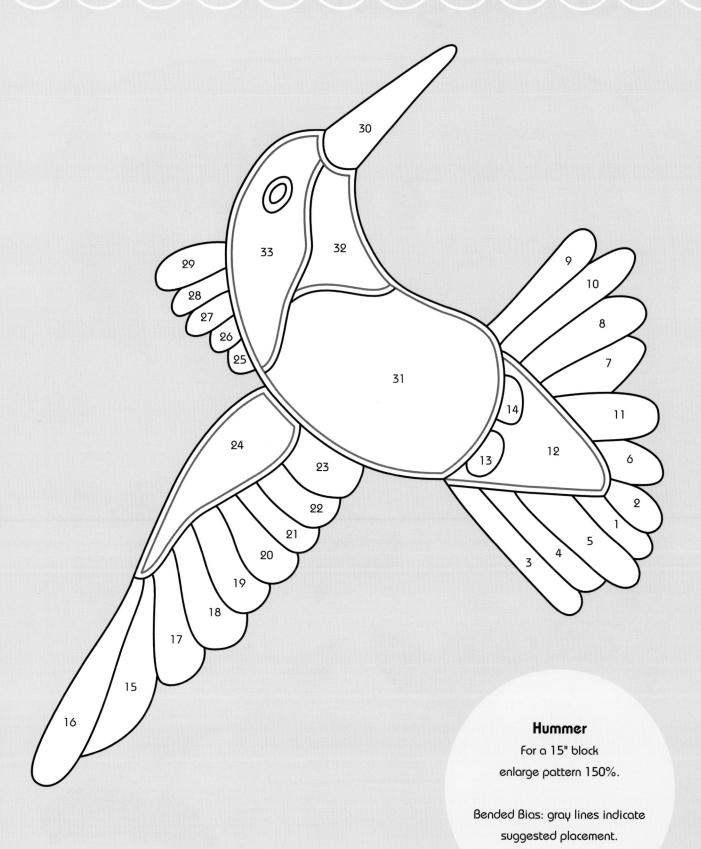

Hummer

for a 15" block
enlarge pattern 150%.

Bended Bias: gray lines indicate
suggested placement.

Hummingbirds

HUMMINGBIRD AND HIBISCUS
52" x 56", detail, made by JoAnne
Finnegan of Dingmans Ferry, Pennsylvania.
Full quilt shown on page 80.

Bended Bias APPLIQUÉ ~ Linda M. Poole

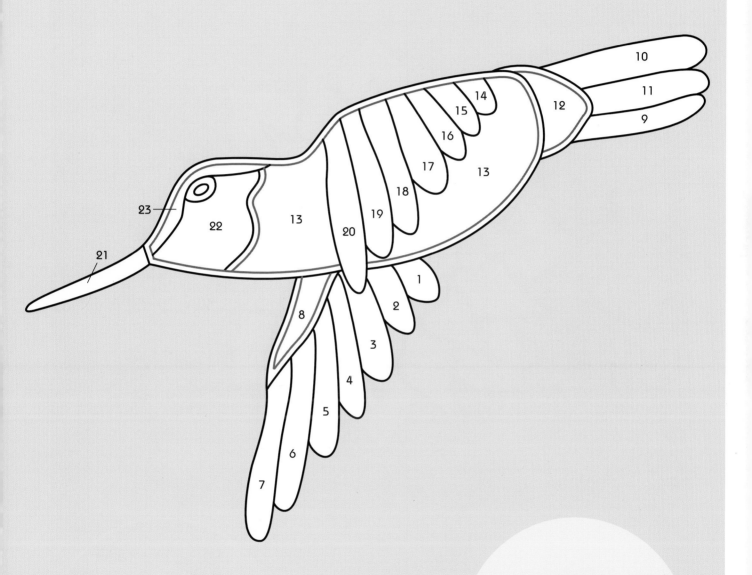

Hummus

For a 15" block
enlarge pattern 150%.

Bended Bias: gray lines indicate
suggested placement.

Sunshine

SUNSHINE QUILT

22" x 22", hand appliquéd by the author and machine quilted by Judy Irish.

Bended Bias APPLIQUÉ ~ Linda M. Poole

Sunshine

For a 15" block
enlarge pattern 150%.

Bended Bias: gray lines indicate
suggested placement.

Sunny Day

SUNNY DAY
24½" x 24", detail, hand appliquéd by the author and machine quilted by Judy Irish.

Bended Bias APPLIQUÉ ~ Linda M. Poole

Sunny Day

For a 15" block
enlarge pattern 150%.

Bended Bias: gray lines indicate
suggested placement.

Sun Flames

SUN FLAMES
22¾" x 22½", detail, hand appliquéd by
the author and machine quilted by Judy
Irish.

Bended Bias APPLIQUÉ ~ Linda M. Poole

Sun Flames

For a 15" block
enlarge pattern 150%.

Bended Bias: gray lines indicate
suggested placement.

Bias Circle

MIDNIGHT CIRCLES
32½" x 46", hand appliquéd by Amalia Emmie Lyle of Lackawaxen, Pennsylvania, and quilted by Judy Irish. Using the Teflon Technique (page 16), you can repeat this design in many color choices, then place the designs next to each other to reveal a secondary design. You can also use just one to make a simple wall quilt, pillow, or handbag.

Bended Bias APPLIQUÉ ~ Linda M. Poole

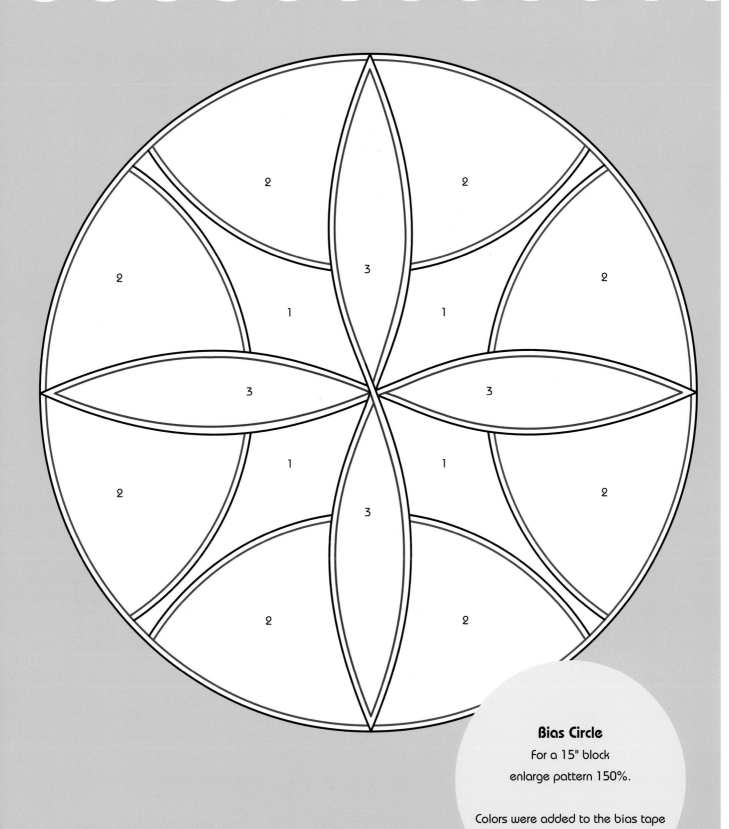

Bias Circle

For a 15" block
enlarge pattern 150%.

Colors were added to the bias tape
lines to help you find your way.

Tropical Swirl

TROPICAL SWIRL
14¾" x 14¾", made by the author.
Use the Teflon Technique to make
swirling Bended Bias designs. These
designs can be stretched to create an
oval border as shown in TROPICAL LILY
on page 34.

opposite page

Tropical Swirl
For a 15" block
enlarge pattern 200%.

Color was added to the bias tape
lines to help you find your way.

Celtic Swirls

CELTIC SWIRLS
22½" x 26¼", hand appliquéd and quilted by Gloria Grohs of Milford, Pennsylvania. A randomly placed cable of bias tape makes a nice border.

opposite page

Celtic Swirls
For a 15" block
¼ pattern is 100%.

Colors were added to the bias tape lines to help you find your way.

¼ pattern

Modena Balcony

Modena Balcony, 21" x 43", made by the author, Milford, Pennsylvania.

Brighten My Table
20½" x 42¾", hand appliquéd by Helen Umstead, Lords Valley, Pennsylvania. While walking through the streets of Modena, Italy, I was fascinated by all the beautiful scrollwork on the doors, signs, and balconies. This table runner is a replica of a balcony made hundreds of years ago.

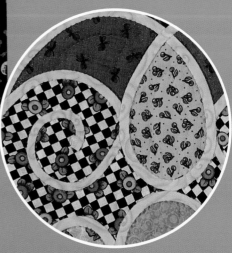

Bended Bias APPLIQUÉ ~ Linda M. Poole

Modena Balcony

For a 20½" x 42¾" table runner
enlarge pattern 225%.

Finding an interesting fabric for the
center helps you select your colors
for the bias tape.

½ pattern

Bended Bias Hearts

In Grandma's Heart Forever
23" x 41", by Judy Brumbaugh, Milford,
Pennsylvania. Here's a fun way to show
off those grandbabies. The Bended Bias
hearts are made by using the Teflon
Technique, described on page 16.

Bended Bias APPLIQUÉ ~ Linda M. Poole

Bended Bias Hearts

Enlarge pattern as needed
for your design.

Bended Bias: gray lines indicate
suggested placement.

Bended Bias Frame I

HERALDS OF SPRING
46½" x 45", detail, made by Helen
Umstead, Lords Valley, Pennsylvania.
Daffodils pattern shown on page 53.

alternate
design

Bended Bias APPLIQUÉ ~ Linda M. Poole

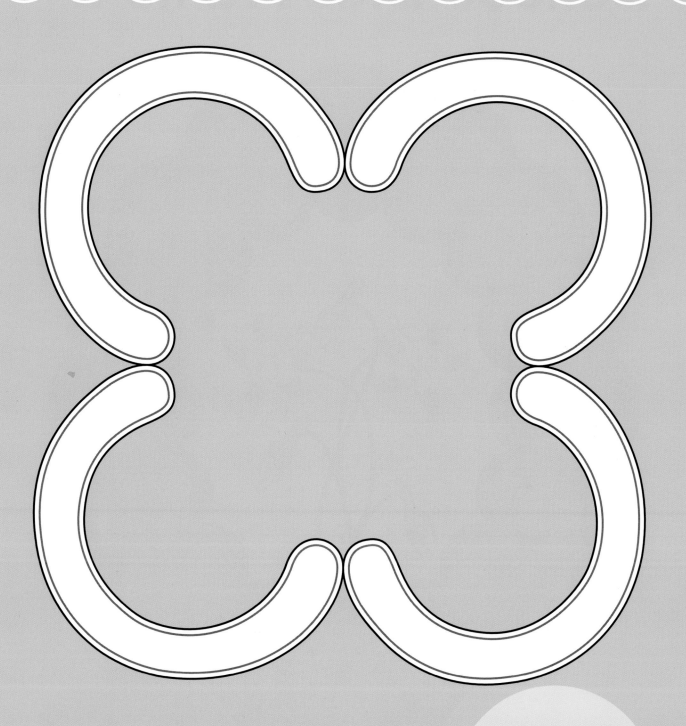

Bended Bias Frame I

Enlarge pattern as needed
for your design.

Bended Bias: gray lines indicate
suggested placement.

Bended Bias Frame II

EGGSQUISITE COLUMBINE
29" x 23¼", made by Jeanne Sullivan of Hawley, Pennsylvania. The columbine pattern is shown on pages 24–25. The border design makes a nice quilt pattern, too.

Bended Bias APPLIQUÉ ~ Linda M. Poole

Bended Bias Frame II

Enlarge pattern as needed
for your design.

Bended Bias: gray lines indicate
suggested placement.

Bended Bias Frame III

HOLSTEIN COW QUILT
27½" z 27½" by the author. This Bended
Bias pattern was also used in SNOWDROPS
IN SPRINGTIME, page 50.

Bended Bias APPLIQUÉ ~ Linda M. Poole

Bended Bias Frame III

Enlarge pattern as needed for your design. This Bended Bias pattern was made with the Teflon Technique, page 16.

Appliquéd Frame I

Purple Starflowers
26½" x 29¼", by JoAnn Musso, Dallas, Texas. Notice that the starflowers are outlined in bias tape. Starflowers pattern, page 36.

opposite page

Appliquéd Frame I

Enlarge pattern as needed for your design.

Smiling Faces
37" x 41", by BJ Herter, Milford, Pennsylvania. Pansies pattern, page 32.

Nature's Beauty
18" x 15½", by Mary Clark, Sylvan, Ohio. Hibiscus pattern, page 30. A similar hummingbird pattern can be found on page 81.

Appliquéd Frame II

alternate
design

Appliquéd Frame 2

Enlarge pattern as needed for your design.

Acknowledgments

Sometimes inspiration comes from unknowingly being in the right place at the right time. This was especially true when I saw an All-Star Review demonstration by JoAnn Musso of Dallas, Texas, at an American Quilter's Society quilt show. I learned from JoAnn how to use a bias-tape maker, and I was off and running from that day forward. She has been a continuing inspiration to me as my good friend and teacher.

Family is equally important to balancing any endeavor. Thank you, with all my heart, goes to my mom and dad, Gloria and Gero Grohs, and my sister, Lorraine, for always believing and encouraging me. Mom is always there at my side, traveling to help me gather inspirations for quilts, and stitching her little heart out in each quilt I ask of her. Dad is right there beside me cheering on any challenge I take, and he lends his own artistic expertise when I need a critique. I love you with all my heart.

I also want to thank my mom-in-law, Audrey Weber, and sis-in-law, Billie Jo Poole. You have seen me grow in leaps and bounds and have held the safety net for me with your hugs and unconditional love.

To Helen Umstead, my other travel companion and good friend, I thank you for helping me burn many a midnight candle, quilting and brainstorming with me. You have taught me strength and perseverance.

Each phase of creating a group quilt is equally important. From the early stages of conception to fabric selection, cutting, piecing, basting, and gathering around the quilting frame, I am frequently reminded of the group efforts of the many dear friends and family members who have put their energies into making the quilts that help these pages sparkle. This book is the frame, and each of you has gathered around to bring my endeavor to fruition. Just as a label on a quilt is important for telling its story, your names, written here, forever tell of your generosity for which I shall always be indebted:

Bonnie Boehm, Bonnie Browning, Judy Brumbaugh, Diane Brush, Mary Clark, JoAnne Finnegan, Susan Gerhardt, Gloria Grohs, BJ Herter, Carol Hill, Judy Irish, Kathy Isaacks, Emmie Lyle, Mary McDowell, JoAnn Musso, Laura Orben, Libby Paul, Jeanne Sullivan, and Helen Umstead.

Thank you forever to my quilt guild, the Milford Valley Quilters Guild of Milford, Pennsylvania, for all of your encouragement and friendships; you have become my extended family.

With the expertise of several invaluable artists, I was able to turn my drawings into illustrations for this book. Thank you dearly Jennifer Hughes of Shohola, Pennsylvania, Jim Meyers of Milford, Pennsylvania, Bill Poole of Milford, Pennsylvania, and Elaine Wilson, AQS designer.

I also want to thank my dear friend, Alison Rumble, Kingston-Upon-Hull, United Kingdom, who lets me bounce all of my creative ideas off her, keeps me organized, and makes sure I eat and not just continually quilt. Ali not only spends endless hours as my web designer, but she is my friend whom I cherish.

Another thank you goes to Barbara Smith, my editor, friend, and book-birthing coach for the second time around. Our shared connection and enthusiasm have made this endeavor a sheer joy that will never be forgotten. Thank you, Barbara, again, with all of my heart.

The staff members of the American Quilter's Society are amazing, and they are extraordinarily comforting in accepting me into their family. I have made many friends within this fantastic group. Thank you for believing in me.

The following companies graciously furnished equipment and supplies to help me create this book: Benartex Fabrics, Clotilde®, Clover®, Creative Grids®, eQuilter.com, Hoffman Fabrics, J.T. Trading, Jo-Ann Fabrics, Marcus Brothers Textiles, Mettler®, Morgan Hoops and Stands, Inc., NeedleCrafts, and Olfa®.

Resources

The Appliqué Society™
P.O. Box 89
Sequim, WA 98382-0089
E-mail: tas@theappliquesociety.org
Web site: theappliquesociety.org

The Fabrics Center
57 Front St.
Port Jervis, NY
Phone: 845-856-2122
Fabric, notions, quilting supplies

Quilter's Attic
P.O. Box 1592, Route 302
Pine Bush, NY 12566
Phone: 845-744-5888
Web site: www.quiltersattic.com
Fabric, notions, quilting supplies

Wild Irish Rows
Judy Irish
24533 35th Ave. N. E..
Arlington, WA 98223
Phone: 360-403-4868
E-mail: wildirishrows@yahoo.com
Longarm machine quilting

About the Author

Linda M. Poole lives in a beautiful region on the outskirts of the Pocono Mountains, in Milford, Pennsylvania, overlooking the Delaware River. She has taught throughout the United States and internationally, across Europe, Asia, and French Polynesia. Her never-ending curiosity enables her to travel, seeking new inspirations for her classes and her quilts.

She is a first-generation American with an ancestry of European artists, weavers, embroiderers, writers, poets, stained-glass artisans, sculptors, and silversmiths. Everyday, Linda is grateful for her wealth of inherited talents and believes that language is never a barrier in the translation of quilts and art.

Linda is the author of *Turkish Delights to Appliqué*, published by AQS, (2002). You can phone the author at 570-296-4172, e-mail her at artist2@ptd.net, or visit her Web site <http://www.lindampoole.com.

Libby's Hearts, 28½" x 25½", made by Libby Paul, Milford, Pennsylvania, quilted by the author

other AQS books

This is only a small selection of the books available from the American Quilter's Society. AQS books are known worldwide for timely topics, clear writing, beautiful color photos, and accurate illustrations and patterns. The following books are available from your local bookseller, quilt shop, or public library.

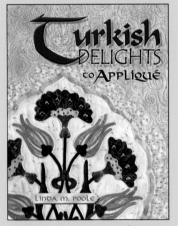

#6004   us$22.95

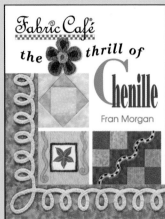

#6418   us$18.95

#6295   us$24.95

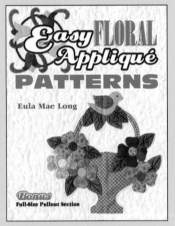

#6300   us$24.95

#6211   us$19.95

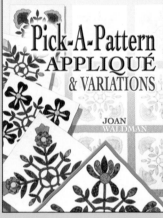

#6077   us$24.95

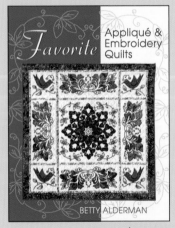

#6410   us$19.95

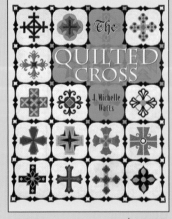

#6301   us$18.95

#5855   us$22.95

LOOK for these books nationally. **CALL** **1-800-626-5420**
or **VISIT** our Web site at **www.americanquilter.com**